THE TIGER KING

The TIGER KING

KALKI

Translated by Gowri Ramnarayan

Illustrated by Krishna Bala Shenoi

ALEPH

ALEPH BOOK COMPANY
An independent publishing firm
promoted by *Rupa Publications India*

First published in India in 2024
by Aleph Book Company
7/16 Ansari Road, Daryaganj
New Delhi 110 002

This edition copyright © Aleph Book Company 2024
Illustrations copyright © Aleph Book Company 2024

Translation copyright © Gowri Ramnarayan 2024

All rights reserved.

This is a work of fiction. Names, characters, places, and incidents are either the product of the authors' imagination or are used fictitiously and any resemblance to any actual persons, living or dead, events, or locales is entirely coincidental.

No part of this publication may be reproduced, transmitted, or stored in a retrieval system, in any form or by any means, without permission in writing from Aleph Book Company.

ISBN: 978-81-19635-32-0

1 3 5 7 9 10 8 6 4 2

Printed in India

This book is sold subject to the condition that it shall not, by way of trade or otherwise, be lent, resold, hired out, or otherwise circulated without the publisher's prior consent in any form of binding or cover other than that in which it is published.

I

The Maharaja of Pratibandapuram may be identified as His Highness Jamedar-General, Khiledar-Major, Sata Vyaghra Samhari, Maharajadhiraja Visva Bhuvana Samrat, Sir Jilani Jung Jung Bahadur, M.A.D., A.C.T.C., C.R.C.K. But this name is often shortened to the Tiger King. It is he who is the hero of this story.

And now, I have come forward to tell you why he came to be known as the Tiger King. I assure you that I have no intention of pretending to advance only to wind up in a strategic withdrawal. Even the threat of a Stuka bomber will not throw me off track. On the contrary, my story may compel the Stuka to beat a hasty retreat.

Right at the start, it is imperative to disclose a matter of crucial importance concerning the Tiger King. Everyone who reads about him will experience a natural desire to meet a man of his indomitable courage face-to-face. Sadly, there is no possibility of that desire ever being fulfilled. As Bharata said to Rama about Dasaratha, the Tiger King has reached that final abode of all living creatures. In other words, the Tiger King is dead.

The manner of his death is a matter of exceptional interest. It can be revealed only at the end of the tale. For, the most fantastic aspect of his demise was that as soon as he

was born, astrologers had foretold that one day, the Tiger King would actually have to die.

'The child will grow up to become the warrior of warriors, hero of heroes, champion of champions. But…' they bit their lips and swallowed hard. When compelled to continue, the astrologers came out with it. 'This is a secret which should not be disclosed at all. And yet we are forced to speak out. One day, the child born under this star will have to meet its death.'

At that very moment, a great miracle took place. An astonishing phrase emerged from the lips of the ten-day-old Jilani Jung Jung Bahadur, 'O wise prophets!' he said.

Everyone stood transfixed in stupefaction. They blinked and looked wildly at each other.

'O wise prophets! It was I who spoke.'

This time there were no grounds for

doubt. It was the infant born just ten days ago who had enunciated the words with singular clarity.

The chief astrologer took off his spectacles and gazed intently at the baby.

The royal infant uttered these words in his little squeaky voice, 'One day, all those who are born will have to die. We don't need your predictions to know that. There would be some sense in it if you could tell us the manner of that death.'

The chief astrologer placed his finger on his nose. Wonder of wonders! A baby barely ten days old opens its lips in speech! Not only that, it raises intelligent questions! Incredible! Rather like bulletins issued by the war office than actual facts.

The chief astrologer took his finger off his nose and fixed his eyes upon the little prince.

'The prince was born in the hour of the

Bull. The Bull and the Tiger are enemies, therefore, death comes from the Tiger,' he explained.

You may think that hearing the word 'Tiger' would have thrown crown prince Jung Jung Bahadur into a quake. That was exactly what did *not* happen. As soon as he heard it pronounced, the crown prince gave a deep growl. Terrifying words emerged from his lips.

'Let tigers beware!'

Of course, this account is nothing but word on the street in Pratibandapuram. But with hindsight we may conclude that the rumour was based on some truth.

II

Crown prince Jung Jung Bahadur grew taller and stronger day by day. No other miracle marked his childhood days apart from the event already described. The boy drank the milk of an English cow, was brought up by an English nanny, tutored in English by an Englishman, saw nothing but English films—exactly as the crown princes of all the other Indian states did. When he became twenty years old and came of age, the State, which had been with the Court of Wards until then, came into his hands.

But everyone in the kingdom remembered the astrologer's prediction. His subjects

continued to discuss the matter. Slowly it came to the Maharaja's ears.

There were innumerable forests in the Pratibandapuram State where tigers dwelt. The Maharaja knew the old saying, 'You may kill even a cow in self-defence'. Certainly, there could be no objection to killing tigers in self-defence. The Maharaja started out on a tiger hunting mission.

The Maharaja was thrilled beyond measure when he killed his first tiger. He sent for the State astrologer and showed him the dead beast.

'What do you say now?' he demanded.

'Your majesty may kill ninety-nine tigers in exactly the same manner. But...' the astrologer drawled.

'But what? Speak without fear.'

'But you must be very careful with the hundredth tiger.'

'What if the hundredth tiger were also killed?'

'Then I will tear up all my books on astrology, set fire to them, and...'

'And...'

'I shall cut off my tuft, crop my hair short, and become an insurance agent,' the astrologer finished on an incoherent note.

III

From that day onwards it was celebration time for all the tigers in Pratibandapuram.

The State banned tiger hunting for all—with the exception of the Maharaja. A proclamation was issued to the effect that if anyone dared to fling so much as a stone at a tiger, all his wealth and property would be confiscated.

The Maharaja vowed he would attend to all other matters of state only after killing hundred tigers. And initially, the king seemed well set to realise his ambition.

Not that the mission was devoid of all hazards. There were times when the bullet missed its mark, the tiger leapt upon him, and he had to fight the beast with his bare hands. However, each time, it was the Maharaja who won.

At another time he was in danger of losing his throne. A high-ranking British officer visited Pratibandapuram. He was very fond of hunting tigers. And fonder of being photographed with the tigers he had shot. As usual, he wished to hunt tigers in

Pratibandapuram. But the Maharaja was firm in his resolve. He denied permission. 'I can organise any other hunt. You may go on a boar hunt. You may conduct a mouse hunt. We are ready for a mosquito hunt. But a tiger hunt! That's impossible!'

The British officer's secretary sent word to the Maharaja through the dewan that the white durai himself did not have to kill the tiger. The Maharaja could do the actual killing. What was important to the durai was to have himself photographed as he stood over the tiger's carcass, gun in hand. But the Maharaja would not agree even to this proposal. If he relented now, what would he do if other British officers turned up for tiger hunts?

Because he prevented a British officer from fulfilling his desire, the Maharaja stood in danger of losing his kingdom.

The Maharaja and the dewan held

deliberations over this issue. As a result, a telegram was despatched forthwith to a famous British company of jewellers in Calcutta. 'Send samples of diamond rings of different designs.'

Some fifty rings arrived. The Maharaja sent the entire lot to the British officer's good lady. The king and the minister expected the duraisani to choose one or two rings and send the rest back. Within no time at all the duraisani sent her reply: 'Thank you very much for your gifts.'

In two days a bill for three lakh of rupees came from the British jewellers. The Maharaja was satisfied that though he had lost three lakh rupees, he had managed to retain his kingdom.

IV

The Maharaja's tiger hunts continued to be highly successful. Within ten years he was able to kill seventy tigers. After that, an unforeseen obstacle brought his mission to a standstill. The tiger population became extinct in the Pratibandapuram forests. Who knows whether the tigers practised birth control or committed harakiri? Or simply ran away from the State because they desired to be shot by British hands alone?

One day the Maharaja sent for the dewan. Brandishing his gun he asked the man, 'Dewan saheb, aren't you aware of the fact that there are still thirty tigers to be shot down by this gun of mine?'

Quaking at the sight of the gun, the dewan cried out, 'Your Majesty! I am not a tiger!'

'Which idiot would mistake you for a tiger?'

'No, and I'm not a gun!'

'You are neither tiger nor gun. Dewan saheb, I summoned you here for a different purpose. I have decided to get married.'

The dewan began to babble even more. 'Your Majesty, I have two wives already. If I marry you …'

'Nonsense! Why should I marry you? What I want is a tiger…'

'Your Majesty! Please think it over. Your ancestors were married to the sword. You may marry the gun if you will. But a Tiger King is more than enough for this state. It doesn't need a Tiger Queen as well!'

The Maharaja gave a loud crack of laughter. 'I'm not thinking of marrying either a tiger or a gun, but a girl from the ranks of human beings. Firstly, you may draw up the statistics of tiger populations in the different native states. Next, you may investigate to check if there is a girl I can marry in the royal family of a state with a large tiger population.'

The dewan followed his orders. He found the right girl from a state which possessed a large number of tigers. Maharaja Jung Jung Bahadur killed five or six tigers each time he visited his father-in-law. In this manner, ninety-nine tiger skins came to adorn the walls of the reception hall in the Pratibandapuram palace.

V

The Maharaja's anxiety reached its fever pitch when he ran short of a single tiger to achieve his tally of a hundred. He was obsessed by this thought in all his waking hours and dreams. By this time the tiger farms had run dry even in his father-in-law's kingdom. And it seemed to have become impossible to locate any tigers, anywhere. And yet, just a single tiger was needed for his purpose. If he could kill that one single beast, the Maharaja would be set free from fear. He could give up tiger hunting altogether.

But he had to be extremely careful with that last tiger. What had the late chief astrologer said? 'Even after killing ninety-nine tigers, the Maharaja should beware of the hundredth...' True enough. The tiger was a savage beast after all. One had to be wary of it. But where was that hundredth tiger to be found? It seemed easier to find tiger's milk than a live tiger. The Maharaja was sunk in despondency. Until one day, came the happy news to dispel his gloom. Sheep had begun to disappear frequently from a hillside village in his very own State!

It was first ascertained that this was not the work of Khader Mian Saheb or Virasami Naicker, both famed for their ability to make off with any animal. Surely, a tiger was at work. The villagers ran to inform the Maharaja. The Maharaja announced a three-year exemption from all taxes for that village and immediately set out on the hunt.

But the tiger would not allow itself to be easily found. It seemed as if it had wantonly hidden itself in order to flout the Maharaja's will. The Maharaja was equally determined. He refused to leave the forest until the tiger was found. As the days passed, the Maharaja's fury and obstinacy mounted alarmingly. Many officers lost their jobs.

One day when his rage was at its height, the Maharaja called the dewan and ordered him to double the land tax forthwith.

'The people will become discontented. Then our state too will fall prey to the Indian National Congress.'

'In that case you may resign from your post,' said the king.

The dewan went home convinced that if the Maharaja did not find the tiger, and soon, the results could be catastrophic. He felt life returning to him only when he saw the tiger which had been brought from the People's Park in Madras and kept hidden in his house.

At midnight when the town slept in peace, the dewan and his aged wife dragged the tiger to the car and shoved it into the back seat. The dewan himself drove the car straight into the forest where the Maharaja was hunting. When they reached the forest the tiger launched its satyagraha and refused to get out of the vehicle. The dewan was thoroughly exhausted in his efforts to haul the beast out of the car and push it down to the ground.

On the following day, the same old tiger wandered into the Maharaja's presence and stood as if in humble supplication, asking, 'Master, what do you command of me?' It was with boundless joy that the Maharaja took careful aim at the beast. The tiger fell in a crumpled heap.

'I have killed the hundredth tiger. My vow has been fulfilled!' the Maharaja was ecstatic. Ordering the tiger to be brought to the capital

in a grand cavalcade, the Maharaja hastened away in his car.

After the Maharaja left, the hunters went to take a closer look at the tiger. The tiger rolled its eyes in bewilderment as it stared back at them. The men finally came to realise that the tiger, in fact, was not dead; the bullet had missed it. It had only fainted from the shock of the bullet whizzing past. The hunters wondered what they should do. They decided that the Maharaja must never come to know that he had missed his target. If he did, they could lose their jobs. One of the hunters took careful aim from a distance of one foot and shot the tiger. This time he killed it without missing the mark.

Then, as commanded by the king, the dead tiger was taken on a grand procession through the town. A tomb was erected over the spot where it was buried.

A few days later, celebrations were held to mark the Maharaja's son's third birthday. Until then the Maharaja's entire mind had been focussed on tiger hunting. He had had no time to spare for the crown prince. But now the king turned his attention to the child. He wished to give him some special gift on his birthday. He went to the market place in Pratibandapuram and searched in every shop, but could not find anything suitable until he spotted a wooden tiger in a toyshop. He decided that it was the perfect gift.

The wooden tiger cost only two annas and a quarter. But the shopkeeper knew that if he quoted such a low price to the Maharaja, he would be punished under the ordinances of the state of national emergency. So, he said, 'Your Majesty, this is an extremely rare example of skilled craftsmanship. A bargain at three hundred rupees!'

'Very good. Let this be your offering to the crown prince on his birthday,' said the king and took it away with him. On that day, the father and son played with that tiny little wooden tiger. It had been carved by an unskilled carpenter. Its surface was rough; tiny slivers of wood stood like quills all over it. One of those splinters pierced the Maharaja's right hand. He pulled it out with his left hand and continued to play with the prince.

The next day, infection flared up in the Maharaja's right hand. In four days, it developed into a suppurating sore which spread all over the arm.

Three famous surgeons were brought in from Madras. After holding a consultation they decided to operate. The operation took place.

The three surgeons emerged from the operating theatre and announced, 'The operation was successful. The Maharaja is dead.'

In this manner the hundredth tiger took its final revenge upon the Tiger King.